The Language Architect: Building the Future with

Mistral LLM

Contents

1. Introduction

This chapter dives into the world of Large Language Models (LLMs) and introduces Mistral LLM, a powerful language processing tool.

What are Large Language Models (LLMs)?

Imagine a computer program that can understand and generate human language like a super-powered conversation partner. That's essentially what a Large Language Model (LLM) is. These are complex AI systems trained on massive amounts of text data, allowing them to grasp the nuances of language and perform various tasks.

Think of LLMs as language powerhouses. They can:

- Generate different creative text formats, like poems, code, scripts, musical pieces, and more.

- Answer your questions in an informative way, even open ended ones.

- Translate languages with impressive accuracy.

- Summarize lengthy documents.

LLMs are constantly evolving, pushing the boundaries of what computers can do with language.

A Brief History of LLM Development

The concept of LLMs has been around for decades, but significant advancements happened in recent years. Here's a glimpse into the historical timeline:

- **1950s:** Early forays into language processing with rule-based systems.

- **1980s-1990s:** Statistical language models gain traction.

- **2010s:** Deep learning techniques revolutionize the field.

- **Late 2010s-Present:** ظهور (chūxiàn - emergence) of powerful LLMs like GPT-3, LaMDA, and Mistral. (Note: This sentence is in Chinese to showcase Mistral's multilingual capabilities)

The development of LLMs is an ongoing process, with researchers constantly improving their capabilities and applications.

Introducing Mistral LLM

Mistral LLM is a newcomer to the LLM scene, but it's already making waves. Developed by Mistral AI, this French innovation focuses on offering a powerful and accessible LLM solution. Launched in September 2023, Mistral boasts several key features:

- **Multilingual capabilities:** Can understand and respond in multiple languages.

- **Open-source availability:** Allows for wider adoption and development by the AI community.

- **Efficiency:** Employs innovative techniques to handle large amounts of data efficiently.

- **Safety features:** Includes built-in safeguards to prevent harmful or offensive outputs.

This chapter has provided a foundational understanding of LLMs and introduced you to Mistral LLM. The following chapters will delve deeper into the technical aspects, functionalities, and future potential of this exciting language model.

2. Technical Deep Dive

Welcome to the nitty-gritty of Mistral LLM! This chapter explores the technical underpinnings that make Mistral tick.

Architecture of Mistral LLM

Mistral LLM leverages a powerful architecture called a **decoder-only Transformer model**. Transformers are a type of neural network specifically designed for language processing tasks. Unlike traditional models that process text sequentially, Transformers can analyze entire sentences at once, capturing complex relationships between words.

Here's a breakdown of the decoder-only aspect:

- Traditional Transformers use both encoder and decoder components. The encoder analyzes the input text, while the decoder generates the output.

- Mistral focuses solely on the decoder, making it efficient for tasks like text generation and question answering.

Decoder-only Transformer Model Explained

Imagine a factory assembly line. The decoder in Mistral acts like a skilled worker who takes various components (words, phrases) and assembles them into a final product (generated text).

- The decoder receives information about the desired task and the initial part of the input text.
- It then uses its knowledge of language to predict the next word or phrase.
- This continues iteratively, with the decoder considering the previously generated text to make the next prediction.

Sliding Window Attention and Grouped Query Attention: Efficiency Boosters

While Transformers are powerful, they can be computationally expensive, especially when dealing with long sequences of text. Mistral uses two innovative techniques to address this:

- **Sliding Window Attention:** This mechanism allows Mistral to focus on a specific window of the input text during each processing step. It's like the factory worker only looking at a limited set of parts at a time, improving efficiency without compromising accuracy.

- **Grouped Query Attention:** This further optimizes the decoder's processing by grouping similar queries together. Imagine the worker

having pre-sorted bins for different types of
parts, making selection faster.

These techniques enable Mistral to handle large
amounts of text data while maintaining fast
processing speeds.

Training Data and Methodology

Mistral, like most LLMs, is trained on a massive dataset of text and code. This data encompasses various sources like books, articles, code repositories, and online conversations.

The training process involves feeding the data into the model and adjusting its internal parameters to improve its ability to understand and generate language. Specific details about the training data and methodology used for Mistral might not be publicly available, as these often involve proprietary techniques.

Multilingual Capabilities: A Global Language Master

One of Mistral's strengths is its ability to understand and respond in multiple languages. This is achieved by incorporating multilingual data into its training process. The model learns to identify patterns and relationships between words across different languages, allowing it to translate, generate text, and answer questions in various tongues.

This chapter has explored the technical aspects of Mistral LLM, highlighting its architecture, efficiency techniques, training, and multilingual capabilities. The following chapters will delve into the practical applications and future potential of this exciting language model.

Leveraging Mistral LLM for Cross-Domain Adaptability

The advent of Mistral LLM has redefined how language models are applied across diverse industries, seamlessly bridging gaps between technical fields and creative endeavors. At its core, Mistral boasts a unique capability: its architecture thrives on adaptability. This chapter delves into how this characteristic empowers it to solve cross-domain challenges, unlock new synergies, and catalyze transformative applications.

Advanced Cross-Domain Applications

Mistral's architecture integrates highly specialized attention mechanisms, enabling the model to understand and generate content across multiple domains simultaneously. Unlike traditional models, which require task-specific fine-tuning, Mistral applies shared representational learning. For instance, a healthcare dataset combined with a legal corpus doesn't dilute the model's output. Instead, Mistral identifies overlapping constructs—like patient privacy regulations—and produces insights that transcend domain silos.

In real-world applications, this is a game-changer. Consider an AI-driven platform designed for interdisciplinary research. Mistral can ingest data from climate science, urban planning, and public health, delivering predictive insights about climate change's impact on urban populations' well-being. This eliminates the need for manually stitching together outputs from multiple domain-specific models.

Multimodal Integrations

Expanding on its domain versatility, Mistral incorporates text with multimodal data inputs, such as images, audio, and structured datasets. For example, in retail, combining user-generated reviews with product images and transaction data allows businesses to predict market trends or customer sentiment with remarkable accuracy.

The model's multimodal adaptability also extends to real-time scenarios. In autonomous driving systems,

Mistral synthesizes input from natural language navigation instructions, visual sensors, and vehicular telemetry to create a coherent understanding of its environment. The robustness of this integration ensures that the system adapts to diverse operational contexts, from cityscapes to rural landscapes, without missing critical details.

Adaptive Memory for Cross-Domain Tasks

Central to Mistral's innovation is its adaptive memory system. This capability allows it to recall prior learning in one domain and adapt it for use in another. Adaptive memory outperforms static embeddings by dynamically recalibrating the importance of learned concepts based on the current task.

For example, a financial analyst using Mistral to evaluate investment portfolios benefits from the model's ability to correlate recent economic trends with historical data. Simultaneously, it applies sentiment analysis to gauge market mood from news articles, tweets, and public statements. This layered understanding empowers decision-making with unprecedented depth and precision.

Ethics and Responsibility in Cross-Domain Usage

While Mistral's capabilities are groundbreaking, ethical considerations become paramount when deploying it across domains. Issues like bias amplification and domain-specific inaccuracies require vigilant oversight. For instance, a model trained on medical and social data might inadvertently favor medical insights over sociological contexts when addressing public health policies. To mitigate such risks, implementing modular ethical checkpoints ensures that the system aligns with societal norms and domain-specific regulations.

Scaling Mistral LLM for Enterprise Applications

As enterprises increasingly integrate AI into their operations, scaling models like Mistral to meet diverse demands becomes crucial. This chapter explores Mistral's scalability, focusing on its architecture, deployment strategies, and real-world applications in large-scale environments.

Elastic Infrastructure

Mistral is optimized for elastic infrastructure, leveraging cloud-native frameworks to handle dynamic workloads. Its architecture supports distributed training and inference, ensuring seamless performance across clusters. Enterprises adopting Mistral can deploy it on platforms like Kubernetes, enabling horizontal scaling with minimal latency.

Take the e-commerce giant scaling Mistral to power personalized recommendations across millions of users. By partitioning user data and deploying microservices-based endpoints, the enterprise ensures the model delivers consistent performance regardless of fluctuating traffic. Each service call is routed to the least loaded node, leveraging Mistral's parallel inference capabilities for real-time responses.

Modular Fine-Tuning

Scaling often requires custom fine-tuning for diverse organizational needs. Mistral's modular design supports fine-tuning on submodules rather than the entire model. This dramatically reduces computational costs and allows enterprises to deploy domain-specific capabilities without re-training the base model.

For instance, a global logistics firm may fine-tune Mistral for route optimization in various countries. Each locale presents unique challenges, from traffic patterns to regulatory requirements. Mistral's modularity allows regional fine-tuning, creating an ensemble of locally optimized models unified under a single architecture.

Cost Management and Efficiency

Despite its scale, deploying Mistral doesn't have to break the bank. Enterprises can leverage its adaptive quantization techniques, which reduce the precision of certain model weights during inference without compromising accuracy. Combined with pruning strategies, this enables cost-effective scaling, especially in resource-constrained environments.

For example, startups in the creative AI space can use Mistral's quantized models to generate high-quality text and art on consumer-grade GPUs. This democratizes access to state-of-the-art AI, allowing smaller players to compete with tech giants.

Governance in Scaled Deployments

Scaling Mistral raises governance challenges, particularly in data privacy and compliance. Enterprises must address these by embedding explainability modules and audit trails into the model. These features allow stakeholders to understand Mistral's decision-making process, ensuring accountability across scaled operations.

In regulated industries like finance and healthcare, such transparency fosters trust. Imagine a credit scoring system powered by Mistral that explains its decisions in human-readable terms. By articulating factors like spending habits and income patterns, it satisfies regulatory requirements while empowering users with actionable insights.

Pioneering Creative Industries with Mistral

Mistral's sophisticated generative capabilities open new horizons in creative industries, from content creation to immersive storytelling. This chapter examines its transformative impact on artistry and how it redefines the role of AI in creativity.

AI-Assisted Creativity

Creative professionals are leveraging Mistral as a co-creator, pushing boundaries previously constrained by human limitations. For instance, authors use Mistral to generate compelling narratives, seamlessly blending genres and perspectives. The model's nuanced understanding of context allows it to craft intricate plotlines and believable character arcs.

Similarly, in visual arts, Mistral aids by generating text-to-image prompts, inspiring artists to explore new styles and compositions. Its multimodal capabilities enable creators to synthesize visual elements with textual concepts, producing art that transcends conventional boundaries.

Personalization in Entertainment

Mistral excels in creating personalized experiences, particularly in gaming and interactive media. Game developers employ it to generate dynamic storylines tailored to individual players. By analyzing gameplay data and user preferences, Mistral generates content that evolves with the player's journey, creating deeply immersive experiences.

For example, an open-world RPG can use Mistral to generate unique quests and dialogues based on the player's in-game choices. The model adapts to the player's style, whether they favor combat, exploration, or diplomacy, ensuring every playthrough feels fresh and engaging.

Intellectual Property and AI

The integration of Mistral into creative workflows raises complex questions about intellectual property.

When Mistral contributes significantly to a creative piece, determining authorship and ownership becomes challenging. Addressing this requires collaborative frameworks that acknowledge AI as a tool rather than an autonomous creator.

Legal precedents and ethical guidelines must evolve to accommodate AI's role in creativity. Artists and developers must work alongside policymakers to establish fair compensation models and protect the integrity of creative industries.

Reinventing Knowledge Work with Mistral

Knowledge-intensive industries are undergoing a paradigm shift with Mistral's capabilities. This chapter explores how the model transforms fields like education, research, and professional services, enabling unprecedented efficiency and innovation.

Revolutionizing Research

In academia, Mistral accelerates research by synthesizing vast amounts of data. Researchers can use it to analyze trends, generate hypotheses, and even draft preliminary papers. Mistral's contextual understanding ensures that citations and arguments align with the latest findings, reducing the risk of inaccuracies.

Consider a cancer researcher leveraging Mistral to identify potential therapeutic targets. By analyzing genomic data, patient records, and clinical trial results, the model highlights promising avenues for investigation. This accelerates the discovery process and fosters interdisciplinary collaboration.

Professional Services

Mistral enhances efficiency in fields like law, finance, and consulting. In law, it streamlines contract analysis, legal research, and case preparation. By identifying precedents and summarizing case law, Mistral empowers lawyers to focus on strategy and advocacy.

In finance, Mistral augments portfolio management by analyzing market data and predicting trends. Its ability to process unstructured data, such as earnings calls and policy announcements, provides fund managers with comprehensive insights.

Unlocking the Next Generation of AI-Driven Collaboration

Collaboration takes on a new dimension with Mistral, empowering teams and organizations to work seamlessly across boundaries. This chapter investigates how the model enhances teamwork, fosters inclusivity, and drives innovation through collaborative intelligence.

Bridging Language Barriers

Mistral's advanced natural language processing capabilities break down linguistic barriers, enabling global teams to collaborate effortlessly. By translating and contextualizing communications in real-time, it ensures that nuances are preserved across languages.

For instance, a multinational team working on climate policy can use Mistral to draft and review proposals in multiple languages. The model's contextual sensitivity ensures that cultural and regulatory differences are accounted for, fostering mutual understanding and consensus.

Enhancing Human-AI Synergy

Mistral isn't just a tool but a collaborator. By understanding context and intent, it anticipates users' needs and provides relevant suggestions. This enhances workflows, reduces cognitive load, and empowers teams to focus on high-value tasks.

Imagine a product design team brainstorming ideas with Mistral. The model generates innovative concepts based on market trends, customer feedback, and historical data, sparking creative discussions and accelerating the design process.

By democratizing access to advanced capabilities, Mistral empowers underrepresented communities and smaller organizations. Its low-cost deployment options and user-friendly interfaces ensure that even those with limited resources can benefit from cutting-edge AI.

Unveiling Mistral's Architecture: Engineering Beyond GPT Standards

The foundation of Mistral LLM rests on a reimagined architecture designed to address the inefficiencies of earlier models while maximizing adaptability and performance. Unlike GPT-based models, which primarily focus on increasing the scale of parameters to improve output quality, Mistral introduces innovations in attention mechanisms, token efficiency, and model modularity.

Revolutionary Attention Mechanisms

Mistral employs dynamic sparse attention, which selectively allocates computational resources to the most relevant parts of an input sequence. Traditional models often suffer from quadratic complexity in their attention layers, but Mistral reduces this to sublinear complexity by incorporating relevance-driven pruning during inference. This enables the model to handle longer contexts without a proportional increase in resource demand.

For instance, when analyzing a lengthy legal document, Mistral identifies clauses critical to the analysis—like exceptions or jurisdictional clauses—while deprioritizing boilerplate text. This selective focus ensures faster processing and a sharper understanding of essential content.

Additionally, Mistral's attention mechanism incorporates a memory-augmented transformer that adapts to recurring themes within inputs. Over iterative prompts, the model evolves its understanding of context without retraining, significantly improving its usability in dynamic workflows like customer support or scientific research.

Parameter Efficiency and Tokenization

Mistral revolutionizes tokenization by moving away from static byte-pair encoding (BPE). Instead, it adopts adaptive token granularity, dynamically adjusting token lengths based on language structure and task specificity. In complex scripts or mixed-language inputs, such as those seen in multilingual corporate reports, this flexibility ensures better representation and reduced token waste.

The model also leverages sparsely activated neuron clusters during inference. By activating only a fraction of its total parameters relevant to a specific task,

Mistral achieves GPT-4-level performance with fewer active computations, reducing energy consumption and improving scalability for industrial applications.

Modularity for Specialized Applications

A defining feature of Mistral is its modular design. Each layer is trained to function independently as a self-contained computational unit. This architecture allows organizations to fine-tune individual modules for domain-specific tasks without re-engineering the entire model.

For example, a hospital deploying Mistral for medical transcription can fine-tune its diagnostic reasoning module independently from the natural language generation layer, preserving general language capabilities while enhancing accuracy in clinical contexts.

Autonomous Systems and Mistral: AI on the Edge

The integration of Mistral LLM into autonomous systems has redefined edge computing paradigms, enabling intelligent decision-making in resource-constrained environments. Whether in autonomous vehicles, IoT devices, or robotics, Mistral extends the reach of generative AI into scenarios where latency and computational limitations once hindered its effectiveness.

Deploying Mistral on Edge Devices

Mistral's lightweight inference architecture supports deployment on edge devices with limited computational resources. Using model compression techniques like pruning, quantization, and knowledge distillation, Mistral retains its core capabilities while reducing its operational footprint.

For instance, in the realm of agriculture, edge-based drones equipped with Mistral analyze crop health in real-time using multispectral imaging data and provide actionable insights to farmers. This eliminates the need for constant connectivity to centralized servers, reducing latency and operational costs.

Real-Time Decision-Making

In high-stakes environments like autonomous driving, Mistral demonstrates unparalleled prowess. The model synthesizes data from various sensors—LiDAR, GPS, and cameras—while processing complex natural language commands. For example, when encountering an ambiguous road sign in a foreign language, Mistral interprets its meaning and adjusts the vehicle's behavior accordingly.

Moreover, its reinforcement learning-enhanced inference allows systems to make decisions under uncertainty, improving resilience in unpredictable environments such as natural disasters or urban combat zones for defense applications.

Ethical and Privacy Concerns in Edge Deployments

Edge computing introduces challenges related to data privacy and ethical decision-making. Mistral incorporates federated learning protocols, ensuring that sensitive data remains localized on devices. This not only minimizes security risks but also aligns deployments with stringent privacy regulations like GDPR.

Humanizing Conversational Agents with Mistral

Conversational AI has evolved from transactional interactions to deeply contextual engagements, and Mistral leads this revolution with its human-like conversational abilities. This chapter explores how Mistral redefines dialogue systems, enhancing their empathy, coherence, and personalization.

Understanding Emotional Nuances

One of Mistral's breakthroughs is its ability to understand and emulate emotional contexts. By analyzing sentiment and tone, the model adjusts its responses to resonate with the user's emotional state. For example, in mental health applications, Mistral can provide supportive and empathetic responses tailored to users experiencing anxiety or stress.

Context Persistence

Unlike traditional chatbots that lose track of context in extended conversations, Mistral employs long-term memory embeddings. This allows it to maintain coherence over multi-turn dialogues. For instance, a virtual tutor using Mistral can recall a student's past questions and learning preferences, creating a personalized and seamless educational experience.

Multilingual and Multimodal Conversations

Mistral supports real-time multilingual dialogue, enabling fluid communication across linguistic boundaries. In addition, its multimodal capabilities allow it to interpret and generate responses involving text, images, or audio inputs. A healthcare chatbot, for instance, could analyze a photo of a rash and combine it with textual symptoms to provide preliminary diagnostic suggestions.

Generative AI in Strategic Decision-Making

In industries like finance, logistics, and energy, Mistral is reshaping strategic decision-making processes by delivering actionable insights derived from complex data. Its ability to simulate scenarios, analyze trends, and provide predictive analytics positions it as an indispensable tool for leaders and analysts.

Data Fusion for Holistic Insights

Mistral excels at integrating disparate data sources, from structured databases to unstructured text. This capability is critical in sectors like finance, where decisions hinge on understanding correlations between market trends, geopolitical events, and economic policies.

For example, a hedge fund manager using Mistral can analyze sentiment in earnings call transcripts, correlate it with market data, and generate a forecast on stock performance. This holistic approach reduces reliance on intuition, enabling more data-driven strategies.

Simulating "What-If" Scenarios

Strategic planning often involves anticipating the outcomes of various courses of action. Mistral's generative capabilities allow organizations to simulate "what-if" scenarios with high fidelity. A logistics company, for example, might model the impact of port closures on global supply chains, enabling proactive risk mitigation.

Automating Knowledge Extraction

Mistral automates the extraction of knowledge from dense documents, such as regulatory filings or technical manuals. This not only saves time but also ensures consistency in decision-making. For instance, energy companies analyzing contracts for renewable projects can rely on Mistral to identify critical clauses related to compliance and risk management.

Mistral in Personalized Learning Ecosystems

Education is witnessing a paradigm shift with the adoption of Mistral, enabling personalized, adaptive, and accessible learning experiences. This chapter explores how Mistral transforms traditional education systems into dynamic, learner-centered ecosystems.

Adaptive Learning Models

Mistral drives adaptive learning by analyzing student behavior and tailoring content to individual needs. In a language-learning application, the model adjusts lesson difficulty based on the learner's progress, focusing on areas where they struggle while reinforcing their strengths.

Enabling Access for Diverse Learners

Mistral breaks barriers for learners with disabilities through multimodal content delivery. For example, it generates audio explanations of visual concepts for visually impaired learners or converts complex text into simplified formats for those with cognitive challenges.

Empowering Educators

Educators leverage Mistral to streamline lesson planning and grading. The model generates custom lesson plans aligned with curriculum standards and

evaluates student submissions with detailed feedback.

This frees up time for teachers to focus on interactive

and creative aspects of education.

3. Capabilities and Applications

Now that you understand the inner workings of

Mistral LLM, let's explore what it can actually do! This

chapter dives into the various capabilities and applications of this powerful language model.

Text Generation with Mistral LLM

Mistral shines in its ability to generate human-quality text formats. Need a poem for a loved one? A creative script for a video? Mistral can craft it based on your instructions.

Here are some examples of its text generation prowess:

- **Creative Writing:** Generate poems, scripts, musical pieces, and even code.
- **Content Creation:** Craft marketing copy, social media posts, or blog articles.

- **Storytelling:** Develop engaging narratives based on your ideas.

Imagine Mistral as a versatile writing assistant, helping you generate different creative text formats and overcome writer's block.

Chatbots and Virtual Assistants Powered by Mistral

Mistral isn't limited to text generation. It can be fine-tuned for specific tasks, making it ideal for powering chatbots and virtual assistants. Here's how:

- **Instruction-tuned models:** These specialized versions of Mistral are trained on specific instructions and dialogue formats. They can understand your requests, answer your questions, and even hold engaging conversations.

- **Improved customer service:** Chatbots powered by Mistral can provide 24/7 support, answer frequently asked questions, and even schedule appointments.

- **Enhanced user experience:** Virtual assistants equipped with Mistral can set reminders, manage calendars, and personalize your digital interactions.

Mistral can transform chatbots and virtual assistants into more natural and helpful companions.

Keeping Things Safe: Content Moderation and Safety Features

Mistral prioritizes safety and responsible use. Here's how it tackles potential issues:

- **Content moderation:** Mistral can be trained to identify and flag harmful or offensive content. This helps prevent the spread of misinformation and protects users from negativity online.

- **System-level guardrails:** Mistral incorporates built-in safeguards to prevent it from generating outputs that are biased, discriminatory, or misleading. These guardrails act like safety nets, ensuring responsible use of the model's capabilities.

Mistral's commitment to safety makes it a valuable tool for online platforms and content creators.

Beyond Text Generation: Exploring Other Applications

Mistral's potential extends beyond the examples mentioned above. Here are some additional applications to explore:

- **Machine translation:** Translate text between different languages with impressive accuracy.

- **Text summarization:** Condense lengthy documents into concise summaries, saving you valuable time.

- **Code generation:** Assist programmers by generating code snippets based on their instructions.

As research progresses, we can expect even more innovative applications for Mistral in various fields.

This chapter has highlighted the diverse capabilities and applications of Mistral LLM. The next chapters will delve into the considerations for development and use, as well as explore the exciting future potential of this technology.

4. Development and Use Considerations

Mistral LLM presents a powerful tool, but like any technology, it requires thoughtful development and responsible use. This chapter explores these considerations.

Open-source Availability and Usage

One of Mistral's unique features is its open-source nature. This means the core code behind the model is publicly available, allowing anyone with the technical expertise to access, study, and even modify it. Here's what this openness entails:

- **Wider adoption:** Open-source availability fosters a larger developer community who can contribute to the improvement and application of Mistral.

- **Transparency and trust:** Making the code accessible allows for scrutiny and helps build trust in how Mistral functions.

While open-source availability offers benefits, it also necessitates responsible use by developers and users.

System-level Guardrails and Output Constraints

Mistral incorporates safeguards to ensure responsible use. Here's how these guardrails work:

- **System-level guardrails:** These are built-in mechanisms that prevent the model from generating outputs that violate pre-defined parameters. Imagine guardrails on a bridge, preventing the model from venturing into unsafe territory like generating hateful content.

- **Output constraints:** These are specific limitations placed on the model's outputs. For instance, the model might be restricted from generating text exceeding a certain character limit or from including profanity.

These guardrails and constraints are crucial for ensuring Mistral is used ethically and responsibly.

Ethical Considerations in LLM Development and Use

The development and use of any LLM, including Mistral, raises ethical considerations. Here are some key points to remember:

- **Bias:** LLMs trained on vast amounts of data can inherit biases present in that data. It's crucial to be mindful of potential biases and implement mitigation strategies.

- **Transparency:** Understanding how LLMs arrive at their outputs is essential. This transparency allows users to assess the trustworthiness and potential limitations of the generated content.

- **Accountability:** Developers and users of LLMs share responsibility for their ethical application. Developers should prioritize safeguards, while users should be critical consumers of the generated content.

By acknowledging and addressing these ethical considerations, we can ensure that Mistral LLM is a force for good in the world.

This chapter has explored the development and use considerations surrounding Mistral LLM. The next chapter will delve into the exciting future potential of this technology.

5. The Future of Mistral LLM

Mistral LLM is a young but promising player in the LLM landscape. This chapter explores its potential for future advancements and applications.

Potential Advancements and Applications

The future holds exciting possibilities for Mistral LLM. Here are some areas where we might see significant advancements:

- **Improved factual accuracy:** As training data and techniques evolve, Mistral's ability to generate factually accurate content will continue to improve. Imagine it becoming a reliable research assistant, helping you find and verify information.

- **Enhanced reasoning capabilities:** Future iterations of Mistral might possess stronger reasoning abilities, allowing them to solve problems, draw logical conclusions, and answer complex questions in an even more comprehensive way.

- **Personalized experiences:** Mistral could be tailored to individual users, generating content and interacting in ways that cater to specific preferences and needs.

- **Integration with other AI systems:** Imagine Mistral working seamlessly with other AI tools, like computer vision or robotics, creating a powerful synergy for various applications.

These advancements have the potential to revolutionize various fields, from education and healthcare to creative industries and scientific research.

The Role of Mistral LLM in the LLM Landscape

The LLM landscape is constantly evolving, with new

models emerging all the time. Here's how Mistral

might carve its niche:

- **Focus on responsible AI:** Mistral's emphasis on open-source availability, safety features, and ethical considerations could position it as a leader in responsible LLM development.

- **Multilingual capabilities:** With its ability to handle multiple languages, Mistral can bridge communication gaps and foster global collaboration.

- **Efficiency and Accessibility:** Mistral's architecture focuses on efficiency, making it a potentially more accessible option for wider adoption compared to computationally expensive models.

By capitalizing on its strengths and addressing potential limitations, Mistral LLM has the potential to become a valuable asset in the ever-growing world of large language models.

Mistral LLM and the Future of Autonomous Systems

Autonomous systems, particularly those employed in complex environments such as autonomous vehicles, robotics, and industrial automation, demand the most advanced AI capabilities. Mistral LLM is poised to lead this transformation, bringing an unprecedented level of decision-making ability, adaptability, and situational awareness to these systems. In this chapter, we will explore how Mistral is enabling the next generation of intelligent autonomous agents, improving their performance, autonomy, and safety.

Enhancing Perception and Decision-Making in Autonomous Vehicles

Mistral LLM's ability to process vast amounts of unstructured data from a variety of sensors is one of its most defining features. In the context of autonomous vehicles, it allows for real-time processing of visual, radar, and LiDAR inputs, while also handling natural language instructions and generating human-like communication. This multi-modal processing capability ensures that the vehicle can accurately perceive its surroundings, understand complex instructions, and respond in an adaptive manner.

For example, a Mistral-powered autonomous vehicle could navigate a busy urban street, analyzing and responding to traffic conditions, pedestrian movements, and sudden changes in the environment while also interpreting the driver's spoken requests for re-routing or stopping at specific locations. The vehicle's decision-making framework would continually learn and adapt based on feedback from the environment and user interactions, improving safety and reducing reliance on human intervention.

Intelligent Robotics and the Role of Mistral LLM

In robotics, Mistral LLM is driving the evolution of systems capable of complex, nuanced decision-making. By processing natural language commands in real time and interpreting visual inputs, Mistral equips robots to perform tasks in dynamic and unpredictable environments. For instance, robots designed for search and rescue missions can interpret instructions from a human operator, analyze the environment, and autonomously navigate hazardous terrain.

Mistral's strength in enabling robotics is also evident in its integration with machine learning systems that enhance object recognition and task execution. In industrial automation, robots equipped with Mistral can autonomously adjust their actions based on subtle changes in production line conditions, helping to optimize manufacturing efficiency without needing constant human oversight.

Safety and Redundancy in Autonomous Systems

Safety is paramount in autonomous systems, and Mistral LLM addresses this challenge by supporting decision-making based on redundancy and fail-safe protocols. In critical applications such as healthcare robotics or autonomous vehicles, where human life may be at stake, Mistral's dynamic decision-making capabilities ensure that the system can quickly assess and respond to failures or anomalies.

Moreover, Mistral's advanced error detection and recovery mechanisms provide a high degree of reliability, ensuring that autonomous systems can continue operating safely even in the face of unexpected events or environmental challenges. This redundancy is essential for widespread adoption in industries such as aviation, defense, and healthcare, where safety standards are strict and often non-negotiable.

Mistral in Healthcare: Revolutionizing Diagnosis and Treatment

Mistral's potential in healthcare extends far beyond simple diagnostic assistance. With its powerful language understanding and reasoning capabilities, it is reshaping the way medical professionals interact with AI-driven tools, paving the way for more accurate, efficient, and personalized healthcare delivery.

Enhancing Diagnostic Accuracy with Mistral LLM

Traditionally, medical diagnosis has relied heavily on a combination of clinician expertise, medical imaging, and patient history. Mistral takes this a step further by incorporating natural language understanding and reasoning into the diagnostic process. The model can sift through vast amounts of patient data, research papers, clinical notes, and medical literature to provide real-time, evidence-based suggestions.

For example, Mistral can analyze a patient's symptoms, medical history, and lab results, then cross-reference them with up-to-date research to propose possible diagnoses. In cases where rare diseases are suspected, Mistral can rapidly explore the global corpus of medical knowledge to offer insights that may not be immediately apparent to the human clinician.

Additionally, Mistral excels in processing medical imaging reports and even radiology scans when integrated with imaging AI. This dual capability helps doctors make quicker, more informed decisions, while also providing second opinions for complex cases.

Personalized Treatment Plans

One of the key advantages of Mistral is its ability to tailor medical treatments to individual patients. Through the analysis of a patient's genetic data, health history, and lifestyle factors, Mistral can suggest personalized treatment plans that optimize for the best outcomes.

In oncology, for instance, Mistral can assist in identifying the most effective treatment protocols for specific cancer types, factoring in genetic variations, the patient's overall health, and emerging treatment options. This personalized approach is crucial for fields such as oncology and cardiology, where one-size-fits-all treatments are increasingly seen as ineffective.

Expediting Drug Discovery and Development

In addition to clinical applications, Mistral is playing a significant role in drug discovery and medical research. By analyzing existing pharmaceutical data, clinical trial results, and vast scientific literature, Mistral can identify novel drug candidates, predict their efficacy, and help streamline the testing process.

Through its ability to process and generate new hypotheses from existing data, Mistral can accelerate the early stages of drug discovery, reducing the time it takes for a drug to go from concept to clinical trial. For instance, Mistral could help pharmaceutical companies identify previously overlooked compounds with therapeutic potential, improving the speed and efficiency of the drug development pipeline.

Mistral and the Future of Content Creation

In content creation, Mistral is driving a revolution, enabling the generation of high-quality, contextually aware, and highly tailored content across various mediums. From written articles to video scripts and social media posts, Mistral's ability to understand the nuances of human language allows it to create content that is not only coherent but also deeply engaging and relevant to the audience.

Generating High-Quality Written Content

Mistral's natural language generation capabilities are cutting-edge. By understanding context, tone, and audience, the model can produce well-structured and contextually appropriate written content for various industries, from journalism to marketing.

In journalism, Mistral can assist in the production of articles by autonomously generating drafts, summarizing research, and even suggesting headlines. By analyzing current events, it can tailor content to the needs and preferences of specific audiences, ensuring relevance while saving time for writers and reporters.

Enhancing Creative Industries with AI-Driven Content

Beyond traditional writing, Mistral has significant applications in creative fields like advertising, video game design, and film. By using its multimodal capabilities, Mistral can generate compelling video scripts, storylines for games, and even dialogue for animated characters. Its ability to synthesize complex narrative elements and ensure consistency across different parts of a story is revolutionizing content creation in these industries.

For example, in video game development, Mistral can dynamically generate dialogues for non-playable characters (NPCs) based on player actions and narrative direction. This level of interactivity elevates the player experience, making games feel more immersive and responsive.

Optimizing Content Strategy for Marketing

Mistral's generative capabilities are also being used in marketing to automate content creation at scale. From personalized email campaigns to product descriptions and social media posts, Mistral can generate a high volume of relevant content that resonates with different segments of an audience. By analyzing data on customer preferences, browsing behavior, and purchase history, Mistral can produce content that is not only relevant but also optimized for conversion, helping brands engage with customers

more effectively.

Mistral in Business Intelligence: Transforming Data into Actionable Insights

The rise of generative AI in business intelligence has revolutionized how organizations analyze and leverage data. Mistral LLM brings deep learning and natural language processing together to offer powerful solutions for transforming raw data into actionable insights, allowing businesses to make more informed, timely decisions.

Streamlining Data Analysis and Reporting

Mistral's ability to process both structured and unstructured data makes it an invaluable tool for businesses seeking to derive insights from large data sets. Instead of relying on traditional BI tools that require manual input and complex queries, Mistral allows for natural language interactions with data.

For example, executives can simply ask Mistral a question about financial trends, market conditions, or operational inefficiencies, and the model will analyze relevant data and generate a comprehensive report. By removing the need for specialized data analysts to interpret and present the data, Mistral accelerates decision-making and increases organizational agility.

Predictive Analytics and Forecasting

Mistral is capable of providing predictive analytics by identifying patterns and trends from historical data. In industries like retail, manufacturing, and logistics, this capability allows businesses to anticipate customer demand, supply chain disruptions, and market shifts.

For instance, a retail chain can use Mistral to predict consumer purchasing behavior based on historical sales data, weather patterns, and social media sentiment. This predictive capability allows businesses to adjust their inventory management and marketing strategies proactively, rather than reactively.

Improving Strategic Decision-Making

Beyond predictive analytics, Mistral assists in high-level strategic decision-making by simulating various business scenarios and offering recommendations based on real-time data. It can analyze financial reports, market conditions, and competitor strategies to provide a holistic view of potential business outcomes.

For example, in mergers and acquisitions, Mistral can evaluate potential targets, analyze market conditions, and simulate post-acquisition scenarios to advise decision-makers on the most optimal course of action.

The Role of Mistral in Digital Transformation

Digital transformation is a key focus for businesses worldwide as they adapt to rapidly changing technological landscapes. Mistral LLM is at the forefront of this transformation, enabling organizations to streamline operations, innovate at scale, and create new business models that were previously unthinkable.

Automating Routine Business Processes

By automating repetitive and resource-intensive tasks, Mistral reduces the operational burden on businesses, freeing up employees to focus on more strategic work. For example, Mistral can automate customer service interactions, handle administrative tasks, and manage inventory, all while learning from each interaction to improve over time.

In supply chain management, Mistral can autonomously predict shortages, track shipments, and suggest adjustments to optimize the flow of goods and services. This reduces human error and ensures businesses can respond more effectively to changing demands.

Enabling Innovation with AI-Driven Insights

Mistral's ability to generate novel insights from data plays a central role in driving innovation. By analyzing existing processes, identifying inefficiencies, and suggesting improvements, Mistral helps businesses innovate and stay ahead of the curve.

Whether it's designing new products, improving user experiences, or optimizing operational workflows, Mistral offers actionable insights that drive continuous improvement. For instance, it can analyze customer feedback across multiple touchpoints, offering businesses new ways to enhance their products and services to meet customer expectations.

Facilitating the Creation of New Business Models

Mistral is not only transforming existing business practices but also enabling entirely new business models. For instance, AI-as-a-Service (AIaaS) platforms, where businesses can lease or subscribe to advanced AI capabilities, are powered by models like Mistral. These platforms make advanced AI technologies accessible to smaller companies that might not otherwise have the resources to develop their own systems.

Through its versatile applications in automation, data analysis, and decision-making, Mistral is helping businesses evolve and adapt to the demands of the digital age, creating new opportunities for growth and efficiency.

Chapter : Mistral LLM in the Future of Human-Machine Interaction

The evolution of human-machine interaction (HMI) has reached a pivotal moment with the advent of Mistral LLM, a language model designed not just to understand text, but to engage in nuanced, context-aware, and human-like conversations. By bridging the gap between machine learning and natural language processing, Mistral offers a more intuitive approach to interacting with technology, making it possible for users to communicate with machines as they would with other humans.

At the heart of this shift is Mistral's ability to understand and generate natural language, which provides a foundation for a wide range of applications across industries. In contrast to earlier models that focused on narrow tasks, Mistral is a generalized model capable of engaging in multifaceted conversations, supporting real-time information exchange, and understanding complex queries. This chapter explores how Mistral is revolutionizing the ways humans interact with machines, enabling seamless communication in industries ranging from customer service to healthcare and education.

Redefining Conversational AI

Conversational AI has historically been limited by rigid programming and a narrow scope of response options. Previous models, while useful, often failed to capture the subtlety and depth of human interaction. Mistral LLM, however, takes this to the next level. By leveraging advanced natural language understanding, Mistral can interpret the intent behind questions and respond in a manner that feels conversational and natural.

Take, for instance, the role of virtual assistants in customer support. With Mistral, these systems are no longer confined to scripted responses. Instead, they can engage in dynamic dialogues that adapt to the evolving needs of the user. Whether a customer is asking about the status of an order or troubleshooting a complex technical issue, Mistral can generate responses that are both contextually accurate and empathetic, ensuring a more personalized and satisfactory experience.

A New Era for Personal Assistants

Mistral's capabilities extend beyond simple queries, allowing it to act as a true personal assistant. For example, in healthcare, Mistral could analyze a patient's medical records, assess their symptoms, and suggest lifestyle changes or treatment options, all while interacting with the patient in a natural and comforting manner. Similarly, in education, Mistral can serve as a tutor, providing personalized guidance based on a student's learning style and pace.

This level of engagement would not only improve the quality of interaction but also offer unprecedented support for decision-making. For instance, Mistral can help managers or team leaders by providing in-depth analysis of market trends, project reports, and even employee feedback, delivering insights that would normally require extensive research or expert consultation.

As these interactions evolve, so too does the potential for machines to become valuable partners in our daily lives, blurring the lines between what is human and what is machine. The promise of Mistral LLM is not just that it will improve human-machine communication, but that it will fundamentally transform the very nature of work, education, healthcare, and entertainment.

Chapter : The Technical Foundations of Mistral LLM

At the heart of Mistral LLM lies a complex array of machine learning techniques that work in harmony to process and generate human-like text. This chapter delves into the technical architecture of Mistral, explaining its underlying algorithms, model design, and optimization strategies. Understanding these core elements provides insight into how Mistral achieves its impressive capabilities.

Transformer Networks and Attention Mechanisms

Mistral's architecture is built upon the transformer network, a revolutionary deep learning model that has transformed natural language processing. Unlike traditional sequential models, transformers use self-attention mechanisms that allow the model to consider all words in a sentence simultaneously, giving it a much deeper understanding of context.

The attention mechanism is a key component of this architecture, enabling Mistral to weigh the relevance of different words and phrases in a sentence. This allows the model to generate more accurate and contextually appropriate responses, especially in complex conversational scenarios where traditional models would struggle.

In practice, Mistral's attention mechanism ensures that each token generated by the model is informed by all other tokens in the sequence, creating highly coherent text that flows naturally and maintains logical consistency. This is particularly important for tasks like summarization, machine translation, and long-form content generation, where maintaining context across a large span of text is crucial.

Fine-Tuning and Transfer Learning

One of the most powerful features of Mistral LLM is its ability to fine-tune on specific domains or tasks, a technique known as transfer learning. After initially being trained on vast amounts of general text, Mistral can be further trained on specialized data to optimize its performance for particular applications, such as medical diagnosis, legal analysis, or financial forecasting.

This ability to fine-tune on task-specific data makes Mistral highly adaptable, allowing it to perform exceptionally well in a variety of industries. Whether it's assisting a healthcare provider in diagnosing rare conditions or helping a lawyer analyze a case, Mistral can leverage its foundational knowledge and then tailor its understanding to suit the needs of the user.

The fine-tuning process itself involves re-training the model with domain-specific data, often with supervision from experts who provide labeled examples. This allows Mistral to learn the nuances of specialized language, jargon, and context, enhancing its ability to produce relevant, high-quality outputs.

Scaling with Parallelism and Distributed Computing

The scale of Mistral LLM requires significant computational resources, particularly when training the model on massive datasets. To meet these demands, Mistral leverages distributed computing and parallelism, which allow multiple processors or machines to work together on different parts of the training process.

This distributed approach speeds up training times and ensures that the model can process and learn from the vast amounts of data necessary to create a high-performing LLM. It also enables Mistral to scale to accommodate larger datasets, improving the model's ability to generalize across a wide range of tasks.

Chapter : Mistral LLM in Business Intelligence and Analytics

Business intelligence (BI) is a rapidly growing field that relies on data analysis and visualization tools to inform strategic decision-making. Mistral LLM is playing a transformative role in this space, helping organizations gain deeper insights from their data and improve the accuracy of their predictions.

Automating Data Analysis

One of the key challenges in BI is the sheer volume of data organizations must analyze. Traditional methods of data analysis often require teams of analysts to manually sift through large datasets, extracting meaningful patterns and insights. Mistral, however, can automate this process, scanning vast amounts of structured and unstructured data to identify trends, correlations, and anomalies.

For example, Mistral can be integrated with customer relationship management (CRM) systems to analyze customer feedback, sales records, and market data. By processing this data, Mistral can uncover hidden insights, such as shifts in customer sentiment or emerging market opportunities, and provide recommendations for action. This ability to process and understand data at scale allows businesses to make more informed, timely decisions.

Predictive Analytics and Forecasting

Mistral's advanced capabilities in predictive analytics are another major advantage for businesses seeking to stay ahead of market trends. By analyzing historical data and identifying patterns, Mistral can generate forecasts that help businesses anticipate future events. This can be particularly useful in industries like retail, where forecasting demand is crucial for inventory management.

For instance, Mistral could analyze sales trends, consumer behavior, and external factors like weather patterns or economic indicators to predict which products will be in demand during a particular season. This allows companies to optimize their supply chains and ensure that they have the right products available at the right time.

Natural Language Querying for Data Access

Traditional BI tools often require users to understand complex query languages in order to access and manipulate data. Mistral simplifies this process by allowing users to interact with data using natural language queries. This makes it easier for non-technical users to access insights without having to rely on data analysts or specialized software.

For example, a business executive could simply ask Mistral, "What were our top-selling products last quarter?" or "What is the trend in customer satisfaction over the past year?" Mistral would analyze the relevant datasets and generate a response in plain language, providing the executive with actionable insights without the need for technical expertise.

Chapter : Mistral LLM in Healthcare: Transforming Diagnostics and Patient Care

Healthcare is one of the most promising areas for the application of Mistral LLM, as its capabilities in natural language understanding, data analysis, and decision-making can revolutionize the way healthcare providers deliver care. From improving diagnostic accuracy to streamlining administrative tasks, Mistral is helping to drive improvements in both the quality and efficiency of healthcare services.

Improving Diagnostic Accuracy

Mistral's ability to process large amounts of medical data, including patient histories, lab results, and clinical notes, enables it to assist healthcare professionals in making more accurate diagnoses. By integrating with electronic health record (EHR) systems, Mistral can quickly analyze a patient's information and compare it against a vast database of medical knowledge to suggest potential diagnoses.

In practice, this means that a doctor can input a patient's symptoms into Mistral, and the model can provide a list of possible conditions, along with their likelihood and relevant treatment options. This can be especially helpful in cases where symptoms are ambiguous or where rare diseases need to be considered.

Mistral can also assist in analyzing medical imaging data. When integrated with AI models for image recognition, it can help identify abnormalities in X-rays, MRIs, or CT scans. This hybrid capability allows for a more comprehensive approach to diagnostics, combining visual analysis with textual data to improve the accuracy and speed of diagnoses.

Enhancing Personalized Treatment Plans

Beyond diagnosis, Mistral can play a crucial role in developing personalized treatment plans for patients. By analyzing patient data, including genetic information, lifestyle factors, and medical history, Mistral can suggest treatment options that are tailored to each individual's needs.

For example, in oncology, Mistral could analyze a patient's genetic profile and the molecular characteristics of their tumor, comparing it to a vast repository of research on cancer treatments. This enables Mistral to recommend the most promising treatment options based on the latest medical research, helping doctors make better-informed decisions.

Optimizing Healthcare Operations

In addition to its clinical applications, Mistral is also making an impact in the operational side of healthcare. By automating administrative tasks such as scheduling, billing, and patient record management, Mistral helps healthcare providers save time and reduce the risk of human error.

Moreover, Mistral can be used to streamline the management of healthcare resources, ensuring that medical facilities are operating efficiently. By analyzing patient flow, staff availability, and equipment usage, Mistral can provide recommendations for optimizing resource allocation and reducing wait times.

Chapter : Mistral LLM in Education: Personalizing Learning Experiences

Education is another domain where Mistral LLM is making a significant impact. With its ability to understand complex texts, generate content, and provide personalized responses, Mistral is revolutionizing the way students learn and interact with educational materials.

Adaptive Learning Systems

Mistral can power adaptive learning platforms that adjust the content and pace of lessons based on the student's individual progress. By analyzing students' responses, learning behaviors, and performance on assignments, Mistral can tailor the educational experience to each student's unique needs, ensuring that no one falls behind.

For example, if a student is struggling with a particular concept in mathematics, Mistral could provide additional resources, explanations, or exercises to reinforce the material. Conversely, for advanced students, it could introduce more challenging topics to keep them engaged and motivated.

Enhancing Educator Support

Mistral can also act as a support tool for educators, providing them with insights into their students' performance and helping to identify areas where students may need additional assistance. By analyzing trends in class participation, grades, and engagement, Mistral can suggest targeted interventions to help students improve.

For instance, Mistral could analyze a student's writing assignments and provide constructive feedback, suggesting improvements in grammar, style, or content. This helps educators focus their time and efforts on high-impact tasks, such as one-on-one tutoring or curriculum development.

Language Support for Diverse Student Populations

In a globalized education system, students often speak different languages or have varying levels of proficiency in the language of instruction. Mistral's multilingual capabilities allow it to assist students in overcoming language barriers, translating course materials, and providing explanations in their preferred language.

This is especially beneficial in multilingual classrooms, where students can learn in a language they understand while still engaging with the core curriculum. Mistral's ability to seamlessly translate and interpret text makes it an invaluable tool for fostering inclusion and ensuring that all students have equal access to educational opportunities.

Chapter : Mistral LLM in Healthcare: Revolutionizing Diagnosis and Treatment

The healthcare industry has always been at the forefront of adopting innovative technologies to improve patient outcomes, reduce operational costs, and streamline administrative processes. With the rise of advanced AI models, large language models (LLMs) like Mistral are playing an increasingly important role in transforming how healthcare professionals deliver care. This chapter explores how Mistral LLM can revolutionize the healthcare sector, particularly in diagnosis, treatment, and operational efficiency.

Improving Diagnostic Accuracy

One of the most promising applications of Mistral LLM in healthcare is enhancing diagnostic accuracy. Traditionally, diagnosing diseases requires healthcare professionals to sift through vast amounts of medical records, research papers, and patient histories. Mistral, with its natural language processing (NLP) capabilities, can analyze complex medical data, including unstructured text such as medical histories, radiology reports, and clinical notes, to assist healthcare providers in diagnosing diseases more accurately and faster.

Case Study: Early Cancer Detection

Consider the case of early cancer detection, where timely diagnosis is critical for effective treatment. Mistral can analyze patient data, including symptoms, genetic profiles, and previous medical records, to identify patterns associated with early-stage cancers. By comparing a patient's data with extensive cancer databases, Mistral can flag potential concerns for doctors to investigate further, helping to detect cancers before they are visible through traditional methods like imaging or blood tests.

For example, in breast cancer diagnosis, Mistral could analyze mammogram reports, patient family history, and lifestyle factors to recommend whether further tests, such as biopsies or genetic screenings, are needed. This ensures that healthcare professionals focus on the most promising leads, saving time and improving patient outcomes.

Identifying Rare Diseases

Another critical use of Mistral is identifying rare diseases, which often go undiagnosed due to their low prevalence and the lack of awareness in the medical community. Mistral's ability to process vast amounts of medical literature and patient data allows it to recognize subtle patterns in symptoms that may point to a rare condition. By leveraging its understanding of rare disease symptoms and genetic factors, Mistral can assist clinicians in diagnosing these conditions faster than traditional methods.

For instance, when a patient presents with a collection of symptoms that don't immediately suggest a common illness, Mistral can cross-reference these symptoms with rare disease databases to suggest possible diagnoses that healthcare professionals might not have considered. This is particularly helpful in cases where specialists are not immediately available.

Enhancing Personalized Treatment Plans

Beyond diagnosis, Mistral plays a significant role in developing personalized treatment plans tailored to individual patients. Personalized medicine is the future of healthcare, where treatments and therapies are customized based on genetic, lifestyle, and environmental factors. Mistral's ability to analyze large datasets, including clinical trials, genetic research, and medical literature, enables it to propose treatment options that are personalized for each patient.

Case Study: Personalized Oncology Treatment

In oncology, Mistral can analyze a patient's tumor genetics and other medical data to recommend the most effective treatment strategies. For example, in cases of breast cancer, Mistral can cross-reference the genetic mutations in a patient's tumor with clinical trials and current treatment protocols to suggest the best therapeutic options, whether chemotherapy, immunotherapy, or targeted therapies.

By incorporating the latest research from clinical trials, Mistral ensures that patients receive cutting-edge treatments that are most likely to be effective based on their unique condition. This tailored approach increases the chances of successful treatment and reduces the risks associated with trial-and-error methods.

Precision Medicine in Chronic Diseases

Mistral also aids in the treatment of chronic diseases, such as diabetes and hypertension, where management over a long period is crucial. By continuously analyzing patient data from electronic health records (EHRs) and wearable health devices, Mistral can suggest adjustments to treatment regimens, predict complications, and flag early warning signs of deteriorating health.

For example, for diabetic patients, Mistral can assess changes in glucose levels, medication adherence, and lifestyle factors like diet and exercise. It can then recommend adjustments to medication, suggest lifestyle changes, and alert the doctor if the patient is at risk of a diabetic crisis. This real-time feedback helps clinicians make informed decisions, ensuring better management of chronic conditions.

Optimizing Healthcare Operations

While clinical applications are vital, Mistral is also making an impact on the operational side of healthcare. By automating routine administrative tasks and optimizing resource allocation, Mistral helps healthcare providers improve operational efficiency and reduce costs.

Automating Administrative Tasks

Mistral's natural language generation (NLG) capabilities can automate the generation of medical records, prescription orders, and billing statements. This reduces the administrative burden on healthcare staff, allowing them to focus more on patient care rather than paperwork. Additionally, Mistral can assist with scheduling, appointment reminders, and follow-up care, reducing the number of missed appointments and ensuring continuity of care.

Streamlining Resource Allocation

Mistral's ability to analyze patient flow, staff schedules, and equipment availability can optimize resource allocation in medical facilities. By predicting patient influx based on historical data, it can help hospitals manage their capacity effectively, preventing overcrowding and ensuring that patients receive timely care. This improves patient satisfaction and helps healthcare facilities reduce operational costs.

For example, Mistral can predict when emergency departments will be busiest, allowing for better staffing decisions and minimizing wait times for patients. Additionally, by analyzing inventory data, Mistral can ensure that medical supplies and equipment are always available, preventing shortages and delays in treatment.

Conclusion

Mistral LLM is poised to revolutionize healthcare by improving diagnostic accuracy, enabling personalized treatments, and optimizing operations. By processing vast amounts of medical data and offering real-time insights, Mistral helps healthcare professionals make more informed decisions, leading to better patient outcomes and greater operational efficiency. As AI continues to advance, Mistral's role in healthcare will only expand, contributing to a future where medical care is more accurate, personalized, and accessible.

6. Conclusion

Mistral LLM represents a significant step forward in the LLM landscape. Its capabilities for text generation, multilingual communication, and safety features make it a powerful and versatile tool. As development progresses, we can expect Mistral to play an increasingly important role in various fields, shaping the future of human-computer interaction.

The journey of LLMs is just beginning, and Mistral LLM is poised to be a part of this exciting adventure.

www.ingramcontent.com/pod-product-compliance
Lightning Source LLC
La Vergne TN
LVHW051658050326
832903LV00032B/3889